The Life of Bahá'u'lláh

Written and Illustrated by Melissa López Charepoo

Dedicated with love to the children of the world

in honor of the Bicentenary of the Birth of Bahá'u'lláh.

Text and Illustrations
© 2017 Melissa López Charepoo

First published 2017. Reprint 2026.

ISBN 978-1-971750-00-2 (paperback)

Table of Contents

Ancestry and Family Tree

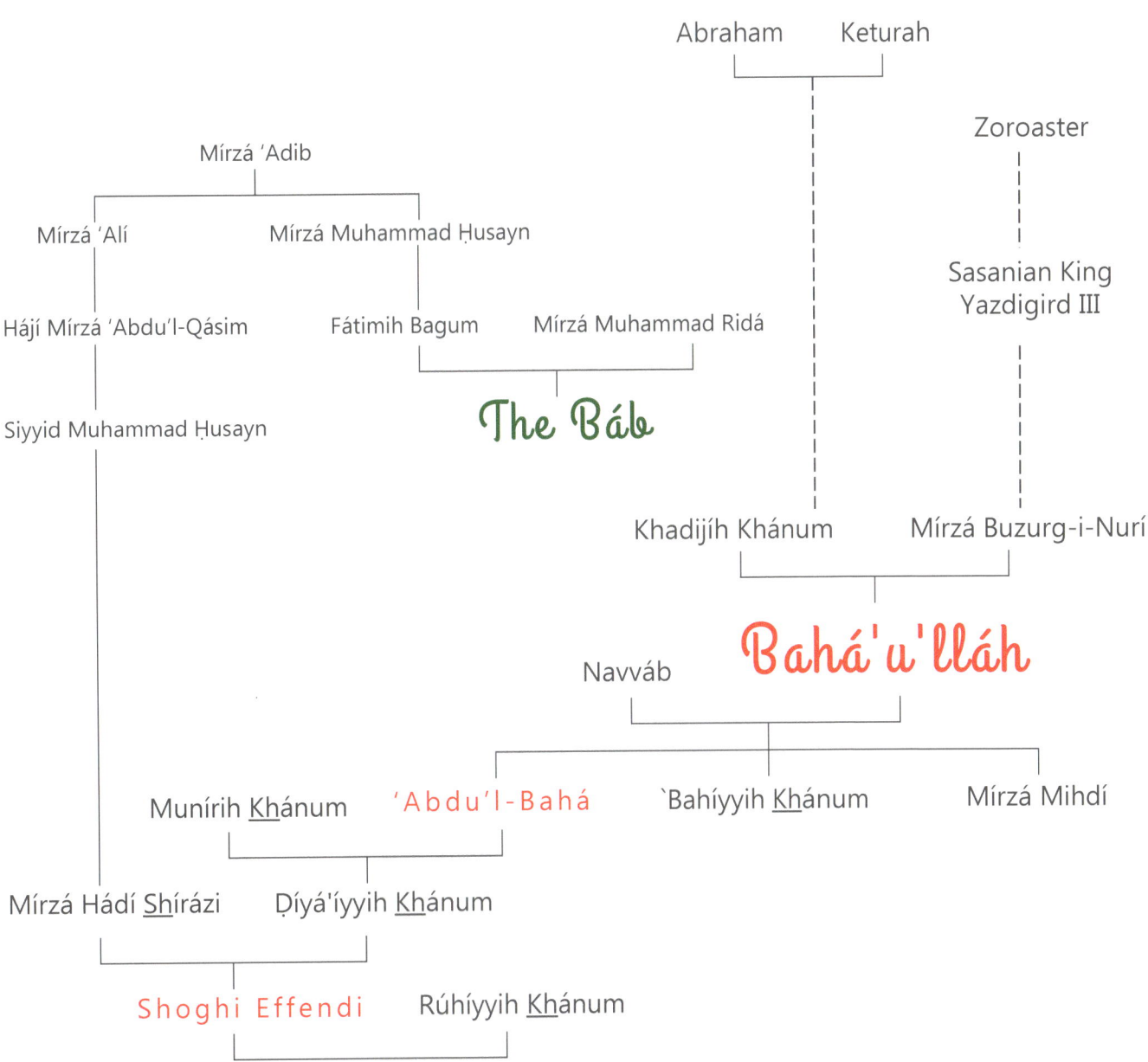

Abraham — Keturah

Zoroaster

Sasanian King Yazdigird III

Mírzá ʻAdib

Mírzá ʻAlí — Mírzá Muhammad Ḥusayn

Hájí Mírzá ʻAbdu'l-Qásim — Fátimih Bagum — Mírzá Muhammad Ridá

Siyyid Muhammad Ḥusayn

The Báb

Khadíjíh Khánum — Mírzá Buzurg-i-Nurí

Bahá'u'lláh

Navváb

Munírih Khánum — ʻAbdu'l-Bahá — `Bahíyyih Khánum — Mírzá Mihdí

Mírzá Hádí Shírázi — Ḍíyá'íyyih Khánum

Shoghi Effendi — Rúhíyyih Khánum

Map | 5

Preface

It was midafternoon, and tears were flowing from the eyes of all who loved Bahá'u'lláh. They had to say goodbye to the Object of their adoration. Wearing a tall hat called táj for the first time as a symbol of His station, He left His house in Baghdád never to return. He crossed the Tigris River by boat and entered the Garden, where thousands of roses were in full bloom. At that historic moment, the call to prayer from the mosques could be heard resonating everywhere.

> **"Arise, and proclaim unto the entire creation the tidings that He Who is the All-Merciful hath directed His steps towards the Riḍván and entered it. Guide, then, the people unto the garden of delight which God hath made the Throne of His Paradise. We have chosen thee to be our most mighty Trumpet, whose blast is to signalize the resurrection of all mankind."- Bahá'u'lláh,** *Gleanings from the Writings of Bahá'u'lláh*

This is the story of Bahá'u'lláh,
The Blessed Beauty,
The Supreme Manifestation of God,
Him Whom God shall make manifest,
The Promised One of All Ages,
The Glory of God.

Birth and Childhood

Birds were singing at the crack of dawn when on November 12th, 1817, Mírzá Ḥusayn-`Alí entered the world. He was born in the city of Ṭihrán, the capital of Persia (today known as Iran). Later in life He would take on the title Bahá'u'lláh, which in English means "The Glory of God."

His parents were Khadijíh Khánum and Mírzá Buzurg-i-Nurí, a state minister of the King's court. He was an offspring of a noble and very wealthy family of royal and prophetic lineage, descendant of the Sasanian Persian Kings and the Prophets Abraham and Zoroaster.

From childhood, Bahá'u'lláh showed signs of greatness. His wisdom and intelligence were extraordinary. He was very well mannered, kind, and thoughtful.

At a young age He learned how to write and read at home but never attended school. He possessed innate knowledge, a profound understanding of all created things given to Him by God as His Messenger. Therefore when Bahá'u'lláh revealed His message, He spoke as God's mouthpiece, sharing with humanity the will of God.

Mírzá Buzurg's Dream

One night, when Bahá'u'lláh was six years old, His father had a dream in which the Blessed Beauty appeared, swimming in a limitless ocean. His body was radiating light, and a multitude of fish started to gather around Him, holding on to His long jet-black hair. They followed Bahá'u'lláh with every move and in any direction He swam. Fascinated by His radiance, they all clung to Him. Unrestrained He rose above the waters, and the fish followed without harming Him.

Impressed by the dream, Mírzá Buzurg asked a wise man to interpret it. The man explained that Bahá'u'lláh, single-handedly, would achieve an important position in the world of humanity. Many would try to oppose and harm Him but without success. Many more would follow and cling fast to Him. He would have the protection of God at all times.

Youth, Marriage, and Family

Known for the excellence of His character and intelligence, Bahá'u'lláh was capable of solving even the most difficult problems. Educated and illiterate alike would seek His advice. After Mírzá Buzurg's passing, Bahá'u'lláh was offered His father's position in the King's court, but Bahá'u'lláh rejected it. He never sought position nor recognition. His only desire was to serve the poor and needy.

A few years earlier, when Bahá'u'lláh was 18 years old, He had married Ásiyih Khánum, a beautiful and joyful young lady from a very wealthy family. She was as kind hearted as Bahá'u'lláh, and soon after their marriage their home became a shelter for the poor. They were known as the "Father of the Poor" and the "Mother of Consolation" because of their compassion for those in need.

In those days it was customary for men in Muslim countries like Persia to take more than one legal wife, as permitted in the Qur'án, the Holy Book of Islám. Bahá'u'lláh had a total of three wives in the course of His life, but it was Ásiyih Khánum to whom He gave the title "Navváb," which literally means "Grace" or "Highness." She was His best confidant, most loyal supporter, and loving companion, and upon her He bestowed the blessing of being His consort (companion or spouse) through all worlds of God.

Bahá'u'lláh and Navváb welcomed to the world a total of seven children, but only three survived to adulthood. Their oldest Son 'Abbás Effendi, later known as `Abdu'l-Bahá, would grow to become the Blessed Beauty's shield, His most devoted servant, successor, and the Center of the Covenant after the passing of the Blessed Beauty. They also welcomed a daughter, Bahíyyih Khánum, and years later a son, Mírzá Mihdí, to complete the Holy Family. For a time they lived a happy and very comfortable life, instilling in their children their love for humanity and service to those in need.

The Declaration of the Báb

Meanwhile on the afternoon of May 22th, 1844, a few hours before 'Abdu'l-Bahá's birth, a man called Mullá Ḥusayn was on a spiritual quest in search of the Promised One.

Long ago, God made a covenant, or pact, with humanity to never leave us alone without His loving guidance. Therefore from time to time He sends Prophets, or Manifestations, to share with us His message. This process is called the Progressive Revelation of God. Now Mullá Ḥusayn and many others in Persia and around the world were awaiting the appearance of a new Prophet of God.

As part of his quest to find the Promised One, Mullá Ḥusayn arrived at the city of Shíráz, Persia. There he met a young man named Siyyid 'Alí-Muhammad, who graciously invited Mullá Ḥusayn to His house so he could refresh himself after his long trip. That same evening, Siyyid 'Alí-Muhammad declared to Mullá Ḥusayn that He was the Promised One that humanity was awaiting. He took the title the Báb which in English means "the Gate."

Realizing that the young man fulfilled all the signs he was looking for, Mullá Ḥusayn became the first to believe in the Báb. After him, seventeen other individuals who were also searching for the Promised One found the Báb for themselves. The last was Quddús, and the only woman of the group was Ṭáhirih. The Báb named this first group of Bábís the "Letters of the Living."

The Báb's religion would only last a short time and would have one main purpose: to prepare the people for the coming of the Supreme Manifestation of God, "Him Whom God shall make manifest." The Báb would be the "Gate" through which humanity would find the path to the "Glory of God." In His Holy Writings, The Báb gave a timeline for the next Prophet's appearance: in either nine or nineteen years.

The Scroll from the Báb

After His Declaration, the Báb gave each Letter of the Living a special mission. To Mullá Ḥusayn, the first one to believe in Him, He entrusted the delivery of a scroll to the "Hidden Secret in the city of Ṭihrán." The Báb did not offer a name but just guided Mullá Ḥusayn to pray and beg God to allow him to recognize the "Hidden Secret." Mullá Ḥusayn followed the Báb's instructions and started his search. As soon as he heard of Bahá'u'lláh, about His character and His devoted service to the poor and needy, he knew in his heart he had found the "Hidden Secret."

And so, three months after the Declaration of the Báb, Bahá'u'lláh welcomed the visit of Mullá Ḥusayn's messenger, a student from a prominent clergy school. The student delivered the scroll from the Báb, in which He announced Himself as a Manifestation of God, the Promised One of the Qur'án and the forerunner of "Him Whom God shall make manifest."

Without hesitation Bahá'u'lláh immediately declared His belief in the Message of the Báb.

Teaching the Faith of the Báb

Enkindled with love for His new Faith, Bahá'u'lláh traveled to Mázindarán to teach the message of the Báb. Bahá'u'lláh was so respected by everyone that soon some of His family members, prominent individuals, and local officials were attracted to the new Teachings of the Báb.

Yet soon a crisis arose, as one of Bahá'u'lláh's uncles did everything in his power to discredit the Blessed Beauty. Out of jealousy, he asked for assistance from a clergyman, insisting that Bahá'u'lláh was taking part in matters that belonged to the clergy and was casting spells on everyone with whom He came in contact. At first the clergyman ignored the matter, but once he noticed that the message of the Báb was spreading like wildfire, he agreed to send two of his outstanding students to meet Bahá'u'lláh.

When the students arrived, they found Bahá'u'lláh revealing an explanation of a chapter of the Qur'án. So impressed were the students with the knowledge of the Blessed Beauty that they found themselves powerless before Him. All their questions were banished, and instead they found themselves instantly vowing to dedicate their lives to Him.

The news of the students' visit spread quickly, and people from all walks of life accepted the message of the Báb.

The Conference of Badasht

The government and clergy were afraid that they would lose power over the people because of this new Faith, so they decided to arrest the Báb in an effort to keep His message from spreading even more. Like all Manifestations of God, the Báb came to educate humanity, and so during this time He revealed a new set of spiritual laws in the **Bayán** to replace the laws of the Qur'an.

While the Báb was under arrest in the fortress of Chihríq, a group of 81 Bábís - amongst them Ṭáhirih, Quddús, and Bahá'u'lláh - gathered during the summer of 1848 in the hamlet of Badasht. It was time to break with the laws of the past, and the Conference of Badasht became the perfect opportunity for it. The purpose of the gathering was to consult about and replace the old laws of the Qur'an with the new laws of the **Bayán**.

For twenty-two days, Bahá'u'lláh served as their most gracious host, renting the gardens, making sure everyone was comfortable, and revealing a new Tablet every day for the Conference. He also gave each one of the participants a new title, choosing for Himself the title of "Bahá." These titles were confirmed by the Báb in later Tablets.

One of the most dramatic examples of breaking with the past came one day when Bahá'u'lláh was bedridden due to an illness. All the friends were gathered in His presence when Ṭáhirih, the only woman participating in the conference, walked in without her veil. This was a very shocking act because the veil was considered a sign of modesty in Islám, and all women were obligated to wear them in public. Tensions arose as some of the men present found Ṭáhirih's action disrespectful to God. Some even abandoned the Faith, but most remained firm, and through the loving guidance of the Blessed Beauty they celebrated the dawn of a New Day.

The conference of Badasht also served as a farewell gathering for the Bábís as most would never see each other again. Soon the clergy and government would start a violent persecution against the Bábís.

Persecution

As the message of the Báb spread far and wide in Persia, the government and clergy, the main enemies of the Faith, started a cruel persecution against the Bábís. Their goal was to destroy the Faith completely.

The crises during this time were severe indeed. In some cities the Bábís were attacked by the Persian army. Some were arrested, while others fled to join other Bábís who were also attempting to escape persecution.

This was the case at Fort Ṭabarsí, where a group of believers gathered in a sacred Muslim place to seek shelter from the persecution. Learning about this event Bahá'u'lláh travelled to the fort to see in what condition the Bábís were. Noticing that they needed food and other necessities, He promised to come back with help. But He was not able to fulfill His promise.

On His way back to Fort Ṭabarsí, Bahá'u'lláh was arrested for being a follower of the Báb. The clergy took the lead, interrogating Bahá'u'lláh and His companions in the mosque. Even though they wanted to put them to death, they instead ordered that Bahá'u'lláh be bastinadoed, a cruel punishment where the soles of His blessed feet were hit with a rod.

All over Persia Bábís were fired from their jobs and their material possessions taken away. Others were arrested and tortured. Many others would be called to offer their lives in martyrdom, including the Báb Himself. He was martyred on July 9th, 1850, though not before sending His writings, pen-case, seal, and ring to the Blessed Beauty.

After the martyrdom of the Báb, Bahá'u'lláh left Iran for a pilgrimage to the Muslim holy city of Karbalá.

The Attempt to Assassinate the Sháh

The Bábí community was heartbroken after the martyrdom of the Báb, but they continued to abide by His message of love, unity, and respect for all. Sadly a group of Bábís were so angry with Náṣiri'd-Dín Sháh, one of the cruelest Kings of Persia, for ordering the execution of the Báb that they planned to assassinate him. When Bahá'u'lláh was made aware of their plans, He tried to stop them, but sadly He was not successful.

One day, Náṣiri'd-Dín Sháh was riding his horse when one of the angry Bábís opened fire. The King was only slightly wounded, as the ignorant Bábí used a pistol loaded with the wrong kind of bullets to fulfil his intentions. Nevertheless, this event fueled the hatred of the enemies towards the Faith and gave them an excuse to commit the most horrible acts of cruelty against the Bábí community.

The furious mother of the Sháh accused the Blessed Beauty of planning the attempted assassination and demanded His arrest. At the time, Bahá'u'lláh was staying as a guest at the house of the brother of the Prime Minister of Persia in a village outside Ṭihrán after returning from His pilgrimage to Karbalá.

His host advised Bahá'u'lláh to hide, but the Blessed Beauty had no fear, as He had done nothing wrong. Mounting a horse Bahá'u'lláh bravely rode towards the Sháh's Palace in Ṭihrán. The officials met Him halfway. They put Bahá'u'lláh in chains and made Him walk barefoot all the way to Ṭihrán.

That day Bahá'u'lláh and the Holy Family lost all their material possessions. They went from being one of the wealthiest and most respected families to living in absolute poverty and being considered enemies of their country.

The Black Pit

Upon His arrival in Ṭihrán, the Blessed Beauty was taken to the worst jail in the country, known as the Síyáh-Chál, or the "Black Pit." It was filthy, foul smelling, and full of crawling animals. There were no windows, and it was cold as ice. There Bahá'u'lláh was surrounded by the worst criminals of the country.

In such inhumane conditions the Blessed Beauty and the Bábís were confined in one cell, seated on the floor in two rows, with their feet in stocks and a heavy chain on their necks. No food was offered the first few days, and there was no place to sleep. Only a prayer revealed by Bahá'u'lláh eased their pain and discomfort:

> **"God is sufficient unto me; He verily is the All-sufficing!... In Him let the trusting trust." -Bahá'u'lláh, as quoted by Nabíl,** *The Dawn Breakers*

So loud and heartfelt was the chanting of the Bábís that even the Sháh in his palace could hear them.

Every morning the jailers would call the name of one of the Bábís to be martyred. After hearing his name, the Bábí would joyfully stand up and, dancing and singing, would say goodbye to all the companions. He then would kiss and hug Bahá'u'lláh and follow the guards to fulfill his destiny. A friendly jailer, who grew to love Bahá'u'lláh, would later give Him a report on how the martyr welcomed death with great happiness.

During the four months that Bahá'u'lláh was in the Black Pit, Navváb and the children were extremely worried. They were concerned about the state of Bahá'u'lláh in such a miserable prison but also were fearful about the possibility that the jailers would call His name next and He would be called to offer His life in martyrdom.

Yet even during such dark times the Faith of God continues to progress through a continuous cycle of crisis followed by victory, a time of hardship followed by a time of joy and happiness, where the forces of injustice and ignorance are defeated through the will of God.

It was in the Black Pit, Bahá'u'lláh's most difficult crisis thus far, that God made the Blessed Beauty aware of His great station. In the darkness of the worst imprisonment, the Holy Spirit revealed itself to Bahá'u'lláh as a Maiden of Heaven suspended before Him, referring to Him as the "Best-Beloved of the Worlds," the "Beauty of God," and promising Him that through the power of sovereignty of God, Bahá'u'lláh would be made victorious by His Pen.

The year was 1853, exactly 9 years after the declaration of the Báb. God had decided to reveal Himself to humanity again, and the Bahá'í Faith was born, though Bahá'u'lláh would keep this event a secret until God's chosen time.

Artistic representation of the darkness in the Black Pit

Exile to Baghdád

Meanwhile, the enemies of the Bábí Faith were trying to do everything possible to destroy it completely. They saw Bahá'u'lláh as one of the most important members, so they tried to get the worst punishment possible for Him: the death sentence. They were unable to do this, however, since there was no proof that connected Him to the attempted assassination of the King.

Next the enemies tried to kill Him by poisoning His food, without success. Finally the government had no option but to release the Blessed Beauty from the Black Pit with the condition that He would be exiled, leaving the country never to return.

The authorities gave Bahá'u'lláh the option of choosing the country for His exile. Although the government of Russia offered to welcome Him, the Blessed Beauty chose to go to Baghdád, a city in the largest and one of the most powerful empires at the time: the Ottoman Empire.

Just a month after being released from jail, the Blessed Beauty, accompanied by the Holy Family and a group of Bábís, left Persia forever.

It was a very difficult trip for the family. Not only were they facing the unknown, but Bahá'u'lláh's health was very fragile due to His time in the Black Pit. Added to this situation, Navváb was pregnant at the time, `Abdu'l-Bahá was nine and Bahíyyih Khánum seven years old. Since Mírzá Mihdí was too young and delicate to make the difficult journey, Navváb and Bahá'u'lláh were forced to leave him in Persia with a family member.

Back then trips were made by horse, carriage, or by foot, so trips from one country to another took a very long time. This journey lasted almost three months in the bitter winter cold, and the Blessed Beauty and His companions arrived in Baghdád ill and exhausted.

Baghdád

Their difficult journey ended on April 8th, 1853. Upon their arrival in Baghdád, Bahá'u'lláh rented a humble house for the Holy Family and the extended family in the old quarters of the city, and soon after Navváb gave birth to a baby boy.

Slowly a group of Bábís made their way to Baghdád. The community was in a very poor state. Most Bábís were confused and disoriented due to lack of leadership. Yet under the wise and loving care of Bahá'u'lláh, the community gradually healed and blossomed again.

A year after their arrival in Baghdád, a severe crisis arose within Bahá'u'lláh's family, caused by Mírzá Yaḥyá, the Blessed Beauty's half-brother. Bahá'u'lláh had always loved and cared for His half-brother since he was a child. With the Blessed Beauty's approval the Báb had earlier named   Mírzá Yaḥyá to be the leader of the Bábí community after Himself. This was actually to allow Bahá'u'lláh to promote the Cause with relative security and freedom.

Yet, after the Martyrdom of the Báb, Mírzá Yaḥyá became so scared of persecution and martyrdom that he hid himself for a long time and changed his name to protect his identity. His cowardly behavior brought much shame to the Faith, and many abandoned it.

Mírzá Yaḥyá eventually made his way to Baghdád to ask Bahá'u'lláh for money to start a commerce business. Once there, however, he grew so jealous of the love the people had for the Blessed Beauty that he started to plot against Him, planting seeds of doubt about the Blessed Beauty's intentions and causing much disunity and pain.

Retirement to the Mountains of Sulaymáníyyih

Bahá'u'lláh's sufferings were so intense during this period, and wanting to avoid becoming the subject of disunity, He decided to withdraw, retiring to the Mountains of Sulaymáníyyih one morning in April of 1854.

There He lived in a cave in the mountains in a state of prayer and meditation, with only the necessary things to survive. Once in a while Bahá'u'lláh would visit a nearby village to get food. The people in this area were usually suspicious and unfriendly to strangers, but soon they started to recognize His greatness. They were in awe of His knowledge and wisdom and started to seek His advice and guidance.

Back in Baghdád, Mírzá Yaḥyá continued to cause trouble. He was living in the family home, trying to control every move and every decision of the family to benefit himself. The little boy that Bahá'u'lláh and Navváb had welcomed just after arriving in the city became very sick and needed a doctor. Yet Mírzá Yaḥyá didn't allowed one to come and visit, and sadly the little boy passed away when he was around two years old.

The death of the child together with the separation from Bahá'u'lláh brought much suffering to the hearts of the Holy Family. The family, especially `Abdu'l-Bahá, begged Him to return home, even sending a trusted believer to plead with Bahá'u'lláh.

On the morning of March 19th, 1856, the Blessed Beauty came home, putting an end to His two year voluntary retirement in the mountains.

Return to Baghdád

During Bahá'u'lláh's absence the Bábí community had reached a new low. Mírzá Yaḥyá had the opportunity to lead them but proved himself incapable of doing so.

Once again Bahá'u'lláh took upon Himself the task of guiding and healing the community. Whether at the public baths, at the coffee shops, or in His own blessed house, every sincere and truth seeking soul that attained His presence was made anew. The community soon blossomed again. The Station of Bahá'u'lláh was becoming clearly visible, and some started to recognize Him as "Him Whom God shall make manifest," the One Who would fulfill the Báb's promises.

Even though He had not yet told people that He was a Messenger of God, after the revelation from God in the Black Pit, the word of God started to flow through Him. When Bahá'u'lláh revealed the word of God, a thousand words would flow out of His mouth in minutes, leaving in awe all who witnessed it. It was during this time in Baghdád that Baha'u'llah wrote some of His most important Tablets, or books, such as the **Hidden Words**, the **Seven Valleys**, the **Four Valleys**, and the **Kitáb-i-Íqán**, a book about the purpose of religion.

Yet, the enemies of the Faith soon started noticing how well loved and respected Bahá'u'lláh was, and how people travelled from near and far to be with Him.

One of them used every means possible to raise opposition against Bahá'u'lláh in both Persia and the Ottoman Empire. He even organized a meeting with the clergy to discuss Bahá'u'lláh's case, with the goal of launching an attack on the community. One of the clergy who dearly loved and respected Bahá'u'lláh opposed. His argument, true to reality, was that the Bábís had done nothing wrong. Instead, the clergy decided to send a learned man to visit Bahá'u'lláh with a series of questions. The Blessed Beauty responded to all of them. In complete awe the man immediately believed in Him.

Still not convinced, the group of clergy asked Bahá'u'lláh to perform a miracle. Bahá'u'lláh clearly stated that men should not test God; however, He still agreed to perform just one miracle, but only if the clergy agreed on what that miracle should be. The clergy simply could not and had to drop the matter.

Thus Bahá'u'lláh won another victory. It had been seven years of great victories since the Blessed Beauty had returned to Baghdád, including the reunion of Mírzá Mihdí with the Holy Family in 1860. But the enemies of the Faith didn't give up, and in 1863 a new crisis would appear.

The Meeting with the Governor of Baghdád

Bahá'u'lláh started to make reference to a severe crisis approaching, thus revealing the **Tablet of the Holy Mariner**, in which He speaks about betrayal and the sadness of separation. When the Tablet was read in a gathering, sorrow overtook the hearts of the Bábís, who feared that they would be separated from their Best Beloved. That same night Bahá'u'lláh received a message from the governor, the leader of the city of Baghdád, requesting a meeting with Him at a mosque the next morning.

At the meeting the governor presented a letter to Bahá'u'lláh from the Prime Minister of the Ottoman Empire, ordering Him to travel to their capital Constantinople and disposing a sum of money for their travels. During these years in Baghdád, Bahá'u'lláh's enemies had constantly tried to have Him moved or exiled to other cities and finally they were successful. Bahá'u'lláh accepted the order to leave the city but distributed the money amongst the poor and needy in Baghdád.

The news of Bahá'u'lláh's sudden exile deeply shocked the Holy Family, the Bábí community, and all who knew Bahá'u'lláh. Everyone was overwhelmed with sadness and grief, fearing that they will never see the Blessed Beauty again. Full of sorrow, multitudes came to say goodbye, overflowing the house of Bahá'u'lláh.

Noticing how difficult it was for the family to prepare for the trip and tend to the visitors at the same time, a dear friend of the Blessed Beauty offered his private garden, so that He could say goodbye in the dignified manner Bahá'u'lláh deserved. Immediately `Abdu'l-Bahá started to make the arrangements and prepare the garden for His Father.

View of the city of Baghdád c. 1860

The Declaration of Bahá'u'lláh

The time that Bahá'u'lláh had been waiting for since His imprisonment in the Black Pit had arrived when He entered the Garden of Riḍván on April 22nd, 1863. It was finally time to reveal His true station as the new Manifestation of God.

"Rejoice with exceeding gladness, O people of Bahá, as ye call to remembrance the Day of supreme felicity..."-Bahá'u'lláh, *Gleanings from the Writings of Bahá'u'lláh*

The days in the Garden of Riḍván - the Garden of Paradise - were filled with joy. Surrounded by roses everywhere, Bábís and non-believers, people from all walks of life came to pay their respects and say goodbye to Bahá'u'lláh. The Blessed Beauty welcomed all the guests in His own tent, served them tea, and with His blessed hands would share some of the fresh-cut roses from the garden that were piled in the middle of His tent. All night long He was serenaded by the nightingales, and some of the believers would take turns watching His Tent.

The exact circumstances of the actual Declaration of Bahá'u'lláh will forever be a mystery, but it is known that the Blessed Beauty decided to reveal His station as "Him Whom God shall make manifest" gradually, at first to only a handful of trusted believers, amongst them `Abdu'l-Bahá. During His Declaration, Bahá'u'lláh revealed three truths about His Dispensation:

- The use of the sword was now forbidden. Violence should no longer be used as a means of conversion or aggression.
- No other Manifestation of God would appear sooner than a thousand years.
- And, at the moment the Blessed Beauty made His Declaration, all Names and Attributes of God were fully manifested within all created things. Much like seasons of the year turning from winter to spring, when a new Manifestation of God appears all things are refreshed and renewed.

The momentous occasion of the Declaration of Bahá'u'lláh occurred nineteen years after the Declaration of the Báb.

On the ninth day of His stay, the rest of Bahá'u'lláh's family joined Him in the Garden. Three days later and after 10 years of living in Baghdád, Baha'u'llah led the caravan as it departed. He was majestically mounted on a red stallion that His followers had gifted Him with much sacrifice.

The twelve blessed days that Bahá'u'lláh spent in the Garden of Riḍván are considered the King of Festivals, and, together with the Declaration of the Báb, are the holiest of all Bahá'í festivals.

Exiles to Constantinople and Adrianople

Victorious after His declaration, Bahá'u'lláh left the Garden of Riḍván in May of 1863 with the Holy Family and a small group of believers to begin His second exile, this time to Constantinople, in a trip that lasted over three months.

But their stay in Constantinople was short lived. A government official of the Ottoman Empire started a systematic campaign against Bahá'u'lláh, filling the heads of others in the government with rumors and half-truths that provoked the call for another exile.

The Blessed Beauty, in an act of bravery and heroism, wrote a letter expressing sharp disapproval of the decision and exposing the pattern of lies, intrigue, and dishonesty in the Ottoman Empire Court. When the Prime Minister read the letter, he remarked that he felt like the King of Kings was speaking to him with God's authority.

And so after just 4 months, Bahá'u'lláh was exiled once again, this time to Adrianople. Without proper food, supplies, or clothing they traveled in the middle of a winter so bitterly cold that in order to drink water they had to first light fires to thaw the ice.

Adrianople

After a twelve day journey, the caravan arrived in December of 1863 in Adrianople, where Bahá'u'lláh and His companions would stay for four and a half years. A period of intense crises began, caused by the powerful enemies of the Faith, but also from within the Faith itself.

The Blessed Beauty's half-brother Mírzá Yaḥyá continued to stir up trouble. This time his goal was to prevent the friends from recognizing the station of Bahá'u'lláh as "Him Whom God shall make manifest."

Mírzá Yaḥyá's behavior became more dangerous when he tried to poison Bahá'u'lláh. Although the Blessed Beauty survived this attempt, the effect of it left Him very ill and caused His hand to shake for the rest of His life.

Yet Mírzá Yaḥyá went still further by declaring that he, not Bahá'u'lláh, was the Promised One mentioned in the ***Bayán***. This was obviously untrue, and so he had forever broken the Covenant of God.

William I,
King of Prussia

Nicolaevitch Alexander II,
the Czar of Russia

Francis-Joseph,
the Austrian Emperor

Queen Victoria
of England

Sultán 'Abdu'l-Aziz
Of the Ottoman Empire

Napoleon III,
the Emperor of the French

Násiri'd-Dín Sháh
of Persia

Pope Pius IX

Tablets to the Kings and Rulers

A crisis as severe as the one in Adrianople could only bring great victories. Bahá'u'lláh continued to gradually unveil the true greatness of His station as "Him Whom God shall make manifest" to the Bábís. During His stay in the Garden of Riḍván the Blessed Beauty chose to share His true station with only a small group of believers, but now it was His chosen time to make a public announcement.

This came in the form of the revelation of the *Súriy-i-Mulúk* and the revelation of Writings that further explained the meaning and importance of the days in the Garden of Riḍván. For the Bábís these were a confirmation of Bahá'u'lláh's evident leadership. Most Bábís remained firm in the Covenant of God, becoming Bahá'ís.

The *Súriy-i-Mulúk*, also known as the "Tablet of the Kings," was a letter the Blessed Beauty wrote to the kings, queens, and rulers of the world. In it He told them about His message of love, peace, and unity of mankind and challenged them to accept Him as the Manifestation of God for this Day:

> **"Fear God, O concourse of kings, and suffer not yourselves to be deprived of this most sublime grace. Fling away, then, the things ye possess, and take fast hold on the Handle of God, the Exalted, the Great. Set your hearts towards the Face of God, and abandon that which your desires have bidden you to follow, and be not of those who perish." –Bahá'u'lláh, as quoted by Shoghi Effendi,** *The Promised Day Is Come*

Furthermore, Bahá'u'lláh sent letters to individual kings and rulers of the world ordering them to uphold justice and to put an end to war and the sufferings of their people.

The process of proclamation of the Bahá'í Faith had started with the revelation from God to Bahá'u'lláh during His time in the Black Pit and continued in the Garden of Riḍván where the Blessed Beauty proclaimed Himself as "Him Whom God shall make manifest" to a handful of trusted believers. With the revelation of the Tablet of the Kings and the Tablets to individual kings and rulers His announcement as the new Manifestation of God for today had been distributed around the world.

Map with the names of the kings and rulers to whom Bahá'u'lláh wrote individual Tablets | 45

Exile to 'Akká

One morning, the house in Adrianople was surrounded by soldiers, who ordered Bahá'u'lláh and His companions to prepare for exile one more time. Due to the constant mischief raised by Mírzá Yaḥyá, this time the Ottoman Empire was threatening to separate the Holy Family. The hearts of the Holy family were full of intense sorrow and pain during this uncertain time.

`Abdu'l-Bahá, who was now 24 years old, assisted His Father with the negotiations. The Ottoman Empire agreed to send the Blessed Beauty and His followers together with four followers of Mírzá Yaḥyá to 'Akká, and Mírzá Yaḥyá with the majority of his followers and some of the Bahá'ís to Cyprus.

The exile to 'Akká in today's Israel was yet another extremely difficult trip for Bahá'u'lláh, the Holy Family, and the Bahá'ís. Without proper arrangements or food supplies they left for what would be their last exile. Some parts of the trip were by land and some by sea. Many of the Bahá'ís arrived very sick, and some died days after.

On a hot and humid summer day Bahá'u'lláh and His companions arrived at the filthy and pestilent prison city of 'Akká on August 31st, 1868. They were faced with the hostility and anger of the people. The government had prepared the population for their arrival, telling them that Bahá'u'lláh and His companions were not only enemies of the state but also enemies of God and His religion. No association with the public was allowed, but Bahá'u'lláh with the vision of the Supreme Manifestation of God declared at His arrival:

> **"Soon will all that dwell on earth be enlisted under these banners." –Bahá'u'lláh, as quoted by Shoghi Effendi, *God Passes By***

The Most Great Prison

Immediately after Bahá'u'lláh and His companions arrived in 'Akká, they were put in jail in an old, foul smelling, dirty army barracks building. The first few nights they were deprived of food and drink, and after that their diet consisted of only three pieces of the worst quality bread a day. The hope of the government was that these harsh conditions, combined with the hostility of the people, would soon destroy the Bahá'í community completely.

Added to the sufferings imposed by the Ottoman Empire was the work of the followers of Mírzá Yaḥyá, who continued to plant seeds of doubt about Bahá'u'lláh's intentions. They tried to convince the people that Mírzá Yaḥyá and not the Blessed Beauty was the successor of the Báb. So unbearable were the sufferings caused by internal and external enemies that Bahá'u'lláh titled the jail in 'Akká "The Most Great Prison."

Yet during this time of intense suffering, Bahá'u'lláh continued to proclaim His Faith far and wide to the rulers of the world. A young man named Badí' was entrusted by Bahá'u'lláh to deliver a Tablet to the Sháh of Persia. Badí' fulfilled his mission but was cruelly tortured and martyred, just as many other thousands had been since Bahá'u'lláh's exile.

Death of Mírzá Mihdí

After He proclaimed His mission in Adrianople, Bahá'u'lláh asked a few believers to travel to different parts of Persia and the Ottoman Empire to share the news.

After learning about the true station of Bahá'u'lláh as the Manifestation of God for this Day, the Bahá'ís from Persia wanted to be closer to the Blessed Beauty, even just for a short time. So they started to make their way to 'Akká in pilgrimage. Yet the guards at the jail would not allow the friends into the prison to see Bahá'u'lláh. They had to be content with just seeing His blessed hand waving at them from a small prison window. Still they returned home with their hearts full of gladness and gratitude and continued to teach the Faith to others.

One day all this changed as the result of a sudden tragedy. Mírzá Mihdí, the youngest child of Bahá'u'lláh and Navváb, was just 22 years old. He loyally served Bahá'u'lláh as one of His secretaries and was very dear to his parents. That day, Mírzá Mihdí was in a complete state of prayer and meditation on the roof of the jail when he fell through a skylight. As he lay close to death, Bahá'u'lláh offered to save his life, but Mírzá Mihdí decided instead to offer it so that the Bahá'ís would be able to come to 'Akká and see the Blessed Beauty.

And so, just four months after the death of Mírzá Mihdí, the conditions of imprisonment changed. The government had to use the jail for its original purpose as an army barracks, and as a result Bahá'u'lláh and His companions were moved out.

Thanks to Mírzá Mihdí's sacrifice, two years of hostile imprisonment in the most cruel conditions came to an end for Bahá'u'lláh, the Holy Family, and the rest of the Bahá'í prisoners.

Leaving the Most Great Prison

Although they had left the Most Great Prison, Bahá'u'lláh and His family were still prisoners of the Ottoman Empire. They were placed under house arrest for short periods of time in different houses in 'Akká, then in September of 1871, they were moved to the house of 'Údí Khammár. 'Údí Khammár was a Christian merchant who lent his house for Bahá'u'lláh's use. The living conditions were tight, with only two rooms for the whole family.

As the imprisonment conditions were relaxed, little by little the Bahá'í pilgrims were allowed to visit Bahá'u'lláh. But sadly this situation soon ended because of the actions of a group of disobedient Bahá'ís. Enraged with how the followers of Mírzá Yaḥyá were still causing trouble, they decided to kill three of them, going against Bahá'u'lláh's teachings about peace and unity.

This brought much grief to the Blessed Beauty's heart and much shame to the Faith. Further, this incident revived the hostility of the government and the population against the Bahá'ís. Bahá'u'lláh, together with other Bahá'ís, was put in jail again for a brief period of time.

Yet, through all crisis and tribulations His Pen never ceased to reveal the Word of God, bringing about great victories for the Faith. When the time was right Bahá'u'lláh revealed the Most Holy Book of the Bahá'í Faith: the *Kitáb-i-Aqdas*. In it the Blessed Beauty established and explained His administrative order as well as the spiritual laws of His Faith and the importance of the Covenant of God and how to abide it:

> **"The first duty prescribed by God for His servants is the recognition of Him Who is the Dayspring of His Revelation and the Fountain of His laws, Who representeth the Godhead in both the Kingdom of His Cause and the world of creation."**
> **-Bahá'u'lláh, *Kitáb-i-Aqdas***

As time went by, everyone who visited the Blessed Beauty was overwhelmed by His honesty and wisdom, so that soon the population's feelings were transformed from hostility to admiration. Proof of this was the relationship with his next door neighbor 'Abbúd, who was also a Christian merchant. He had originally reinforced the wall that divided his house from the house of 'Údí Khammár, where Bahá'u'lláh and His family were staying. But after being in contact with the Supreme Manifestation of God, his heart was transformed. 'Abbúd eventually opened a hole in the reinforced wall and offered a room to Bahá'u'lláh so that `Abdu'l-Bahá would have a place to live after His marriage to Munírih Khánum.

Mazra'ih

One day `Abdu'l-Bahá overheard His Father expressing how much He missed the countryside, which He had not been able to enjoy during His nine years in 'Akká. Immediately `Abdu'l-Bahá started to look for a more suitable place for the Blessed Beauty, finding Mazra'ih, a small house a few miles outside the city.

Although in the beginning Bahá'u'lláh refused to leave 'Akká, as He was still a prisoner, He accepted to move to Mazra'ih after a well-known Arab man with considerable influence humbly begged Him to leave the prison city and enjoy the countryside.

At Mazra'ih the Blessed Beauty dedicated His days to the revelation of the Word of God. Many Tablets of guidance to the Bahá'ís in Persia were sent out during this time. He also welcomed the pilgrims who with love and adoration had traveled many miles and crossed countries and continents to fulfill their hearts' desire of attaining the presence of the Glory of God.

`Abdu'l-Bahá stayed in 'Akká with His immediate family, taking care of the affairs of the Bahá'í community, serving those in need, welcoming the pilgrims, and meeting with dignitaries, clergy, and other important personalities of the area. He continued to serve as a shield for His Father, as He had since the days of Adrianople. `Abdu'l-Bahá loved and missed His Father very much and would visit Him as much as He could.

Riḍván Garden

In Persia the persecution of the Bahá'ís continued with the same intensity. Bahá'ís bravely faced their challenges and joyfully would offer their lives in martyrdom, fueling the growth of the Faith.

Meanwhile in the Ottoman Empire the station and authority of Bahá'u'lláh as a Manifestation of God became more apparent to friends and enemies alike. His grandeur, glory, and splendor would leave all in awe and transform every heart with whom He came in contact.

From time to time, the Blessed Beauty would visit a garden `Abdu'l-Bahá had rented for Him and stay there for a few days at a time.

The garden was a beautiful place with a small island surrounded by rivers and a fountain in the middle of it. Bahá'u'lláh named it Riḍván, which in English means "paradise." There, in an utter state of prayer and meditation, He would reveal the Word of God and also occasionally welcome pilgrims to nurture their hearts with His love.

Visits to Haifa

Although the Báb and Bahá'u'lláh never met in person, as Manifestations of God they shared a bond that our minds will never fully comprehend. Even though they both founded their own religions and revealed their own Sacred Books, the Báb's mission was to prepare the people of the world for "Him Whom God shall make manifest": Bahá'u'lláh. It was the first time in religious history that a Manifestation of God served as Herald of another Manifestation of God, making their religions one. Together they are known as the "Twin Manifestations of God."

The blessed remains of the Báb, together with the remains of His companion Anís, had been rescued and hidden after His martyrdom in 1850. Under the guidance of Bahá'u'lláh - and later `Abdu'l-Bahá - the remains were moved over land and sea on a journey that lasted 59 years. Many years after Baha'u'llah's passing the Báb's remains were at last brought to Haifa, near 'Akká, where they would reach their final resting place.

Years before, the Blessed Beauty had visited the city of Haifa four times in order to choose the perfect spot, pitching His blessed tent on the skirts of Mount Carmel. There He revealed the **Tablet of Carmel**, highlighting the bounties and blessings of this mountain, which is a Holy Place for all of the Abrahamic religions.

It was on one of these visits that Bahá'u'lláh showed `Abdu'l-Bahá where the Shrine of the Báb should be constructed. After the passing of the Blessed Beauty, `Abdu'l-Baha fulfilled His commandment, purchasing the land and building the inner sanctuary where the blessed remains of the Báb would be buried in 1909. Under Shoghi Effendi, the Guardian of the Faith, the Shrine of the Báb was completed as we know it today. This sacred spot now serves as the center and focal point of beautiful gardens with nineteen terraces adoring the holy mountain.

The Mansion of Bahjí

`Abdu'l-Bahá was always looking for ways to make His Father's life more comfortable and dignified, in accordance with what Bahá'u'lláh's station deserved. He found the Mansion of Bahjí, a large house in the outskirts of 'Akká that was also owned by 'Údí Khammár but had been abandoned after a plague invaded the city. `Abdu'l-Bahá made it possible for Bahá'u'lláh to move there by first renting the house in 1879, and later purchasing it, thanks to the generous donations from the Bahá'ís.

It was a beautiful house surrounded by the countryside Bahá'u'lláh so dearly loved. There the Blessed Beauty passed the last years of His life in modest comfort. Left behind were all the years of cruel imprisonments and difficult exiles. Although Bahá'u'lláh was technically still a prisoner, in reality He was loved and respected like a king by everyone. The hostile behavior of the population had completely changed.

In the Mansion of Bahjí, the days of the Blessed Beauty were dedicated to welcoming pilgrims and important guests, like city officials, who sought His wise advice. One of these important visitors who had the bounty of meeting Bahá'u'lláh was Professor Edward Granville Browne of Cambridge University. During his interview, Professor Browne was in awe of Bahá'u'lláh's knowledge, authority, power, and with how the Blessed Beauty seemed to see inside one's soul. So impressed was he that he bowed himself in front of Bahá'u'lláh as a sign of respect for His elevated station.

The last book of the thousands of Tablets and books that Bahá'u'lláh revealed was the ***Epistle to the Son of the Wolf.*** The book was addressed to the son of the clergyman who had ordered the execution of two Bahá'ís in Iṣfahán. In this book, Bahá'u'lláh taught us about the most important principle of His Dispensation: unity. On the unity of the Divine Manifestations He wrote:

> **"The Divine Messengers have been sent down, and their Books were revealed, for the purpose of promoting the knowledge of God, and of furthering unity and fellowship amongst men." – Bahá'u'lláh,** *Epistle to the Son of the Wolf*

And on the unity of humanity:

> **"Ye are the fruits of one tree, and the leaves of one branch. Deal ye one with another with the utmost love and harmony, with friendliness and fellowship." –Bahá'u'lláh,** *Epistle of the Son of the Wolf*

Ascension

Nine months before His passing Bahá'u'lláh expressed His desire to depart from this world. He was in His 75th year of life when at the beginning of May 1892, He became ill with fever. Interviews and meetings with the Blessed Beauty were suspended to allow Him to heal properly.

As His physical health continued to deteriorate, Bahá'u'lláh called His family and some of the Bahá'ís to His presence. Everyone was extremely sad and heartbroken as they knew this was a farewell meeting. He praised them for their service and shared how pleased He was with all of them. He concluded by directing all to turn to `Abdu'l-Bahá for guidance after His passing.

The Blessed Beauty in His **Will and Testament** appointed `Abdu'l-Bahá, the perfect exemplar of His teachings, as the Center of the Covenant and sole interpreter of His Writings. By doing so, Bahá'u'lláh fulfilled the promise of never leaving the Bahá'í community without guidance, thereby protecting the unity of His followers. This is a first in religious history, as most communities split soon after the death of the Founder because they couldn't agree on who the leader should be.

Bahá'u'lláh passed away peacefully at 1 am on May 29th, 1892, putting an end to forty glorious years of continuous revelation of the Word of God.

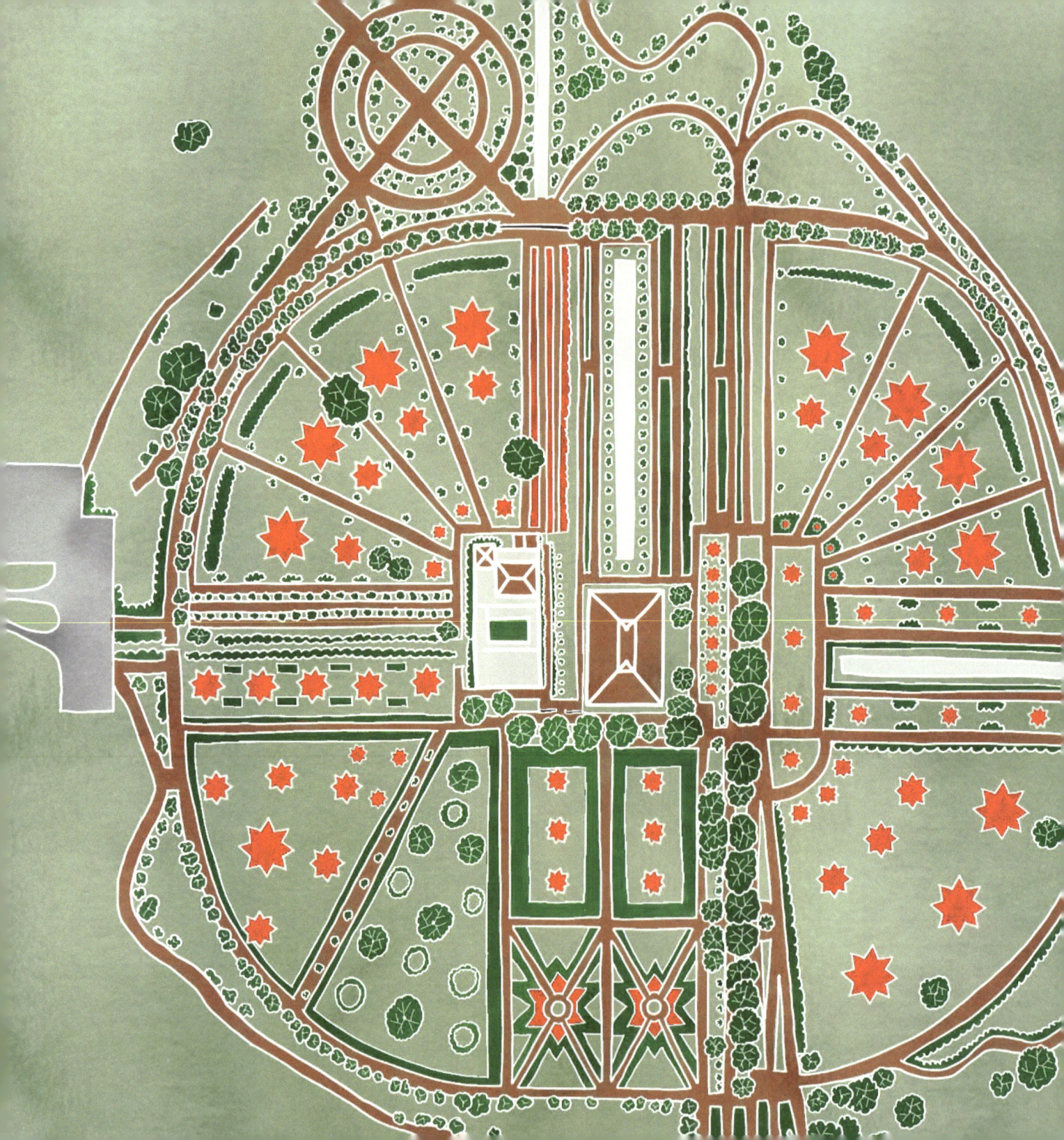

On the Bicentenary of the Birth of Bahá'u'lláh

With the words **"the Sun of Bahá has set"** `Abdu'l-Bahá communicated to the Sulṭán the news of the ascension of the Blessed Beauty. After thirty-nine years and four exiles, Bahá'u'lláh was still a prisoner of the Ottoman Empire when He passed away.

On the same day of His ascension, Bahá'u'lláh's blessed body was buried in a small room in the house adjacent to the Mansion of Bahjí. People from all walks of life - in the city, in adjacent countries, and in many parts of the world - mourned His passing. Rushing to pay their respects, thousands of people flooded the grounds of the Mansion of Bahjí. These were days of extreme sadness for all of those who respected, loved, and adored Him.

The sacred place where the Blessed Beauty's earthly remains were laid to rest is considered the Qiblih, or point of adoration, for the Bahá'í world. When Bahá'ís recite our obligatory prayer we turn towards this spot, which is the holiest place on earth. Surrounding the Shrine of Bahá'u'lláh is the Ḥaram-i-Aqdas, or "Holy Court," a beautiful circular garden that provides an appropriate and dignified approach to the Shrine.

At the time of the ascension of the Blessed Beauty the Bahá'í Faith had grown from Iran to Iraq, Palestine (today known as Israel), India, Russia, Syria, and Egypt. Today, 200 years after the birth of the Blessed Beauty, His message of the oneness of God, the oneness of religion, the oneness of humanity, the equality between men and woman, the harmony between science and religion, the individual investigation of truth, and the importance of spiritual and material education has reached every country in the world.

His Covenant, made up of a line of succession from `Abdu'l-Bahá to the Guardian and the Universal House of Justice, has preserved the unity of a vibrant, ever-growing community, rich in its diversity yet unified in its goal of the spiritual and social transformation of the world.

Timeline

November 12, 1817	Birth of Bahá'u'lláh
1823	Mírzá Buzurg's dream
October 1835	Marriage of Bahá'u'lláh to Navváb
1839	Passing of Mírzá Buzurg, Bahá'u'lláh is offered his position in the Persian King's Court
May 22, 1844	Declaration of the Báb
May 23, 1844	The birth of `Abdu'l-Bahá
1844	The Báb gives Mullá Ḥusayn the task of delivering a scroll to Bahá'u'lláh in Ṭihrán
1846	The birth of Bahíyyih Khánum
1848	The birth of Mírzá Mihdí
June –July 1848	The Conference of Badasht
1848	Bahá'u'lláh visits Fort Ṭabarsí
	Bahá'u'lláh is arrested and bastinadoed
July 9, 1850	Martyrdom of the Báb
1851	Bahá'u'lláh arrives in Karbalá via Baghdád on His Muslim pilgrimage
1852	The attempt to assassinate the Sháh
August 1852	Bahá'u'lláh is arrested then taken to the Black Pit
October 1852	God reveals Himself to Bahá'u'lláh in the Black Pit
December 1852	Bahá'u'lláh is released from the Black Pit
January 12, 1853	Bahá'u'lláh is exiled to Baghdád
April 8, 1853	Bahá'u'lláh and His family arrive in Baghdád
1853	Mírzá Yaḥyá joins Bahá'u'lláh in Baghdád
April 10, 1854	Bahá'u'lláh leaves for the mountains of Sulaymáníyyih
March 19, 1856	Bahá'u'lláh returns from Sulaymáníyyih
1856	Bahá'u'lláh reveals the **Seven Valleys**
1857	Bahá'u'lláh reveals the **Four Valleys**
1858	Bahá'u'lláh reveals the **Hidden Words**
1860	Mírzá Mihdí, the son of Bahá'u'lláh, joins his family in Baghdád
1862	Bahá'u'lláh reveals the **Kitáb-i-Íqán**
March 26, 1863	Bahá'u'lláh reveals the **Tablet of the Holy Mariner**

March 27, 1863	Bahá'u'lláh meets the governor of Baghdád and is exiled to Constantinople
April 22, 1863	First day of Riḍván
April 30, 1863	Ninth day of Riḍván, Bahá'u'lláh's family joins Him in the Garden
May 3, 1863	Twelfth Day Riḍván, Bahá'u'lláh leaves the Garden of Riḍván for Constantinople
August 16, 1863	Bahá'u'lláh and His companions arrive in Constantinople
December 1, 1863	Bahá'u'lláh is exiled to Adrianople
December 12, 1863	Bahá'u'lláh and His companions arrive in Adrianople
1863	Bahá'u'lláh reveals the **Súriy-Mulúk**, the Tablet to the Kings
December 1864	Mírzá Yaḥyá tries to poison Bahá'u'lláh
August 12, 1868	Bahá'u'lláh and His companions leave Adrianople for exile in `Akká
August 31, 1868	Bahá'u'lláh and His companions arrive in `Akká
1869	First pilgrims arrive in `Akká to see Bahá'u'lláh
July 1869	Badí' delivers the Tablet of Bahá'u'lláh to the Persian King
June 30, 1870	Death of Mírzá Mihdí
October 1870	Bahá'u'lláh leaves the Most Great Prison
September 1871	Bahá'u'lláh is moved to the house of `Údí Khammár in `Akká
January 22, 1872	Three followers of Mírzá Yaḥyá are killed by seven Bahá'ís
1873	Bahá'u'lláh reveals the **Kitáb-i-Aqdas**
March 8, 1873	Marriage of `Abdu'l-Bahá to Muním Khánum
1873	Bahá'u'lláh acquires the house of `Abbúd
June 1877	Bahá'u'lláh moves to Mazra`ih
	First visit of Bahá'u'lláh to the Riḍván Garden outside `Akká
September 1879	Bahá'u'lláh moves to the mansion of Bahjí
1886	The death of Navváb
April 1890	Professor E. G. Browne's interview with Bahá'u'lláh at Bahjí
1891	Last visit to Haifa, Bahá'u'lláh points out to `Abdu'l-Bahá the site for the Shrine of the Báb
	Bahá'u'lláh reveals the **Epistle to the Son of the Wolf**
May 8, 1892	Bahá'u'lláh falls ill with a slight fever
May 29, 1892	The Ascension of Bahá'u'lláh

Glossary

Abrahamic religions - Denoting any or all of the religions (Judaism, Christianity, Islám, Bábí Faith, and Bahá'í Faith) that revere Abraham, the Biblical patriarch.

army barrack – A building or set of buildings that provides soldiers with accommodation.

Bábí - A follower of the Báb and His religion.

Bahá'í - A follower of Bahá'u'lláh and His religion.

bastinado - A form of punishment or torture that involves caning the soles of someone's feet.

bestow - Confer or present an honor, right, or gift to someone.

caravan – Historically, a group of people travelling together across long distances.

consort - A wife, husband, or companion, in particular the spouse of a reigning monarch.

Covenant - An agreement. The Covenant of God refers to the agreement that God had made with humanity to never leave us without His spiritual guidance, through periodically sending His Messengers, or Manifestations of God, to share His message with us.

crisis - A time of intense difficulty or danger. A time when a difficult or important decision must be made.

declaration - A formal or explicit statement or announcement.

dispensation - A political, religious, or social system prevailing at a particular time. Bahá'u'lláh's Dispensation refers to His religion.

exile - The state of being barred from one's native country, typically for political or punitive reasons.

execution - Capital punishment, being put to death.

governor – A government official appointed or elected to govern a town or region.

hamlet - A small settlement, generally smaller than a village.

herald - A person or thing viewed as a sign that something is about to happen. The Báb was the Herald of Bahá'u'lláh.

innate knowledge – Knowledge that a person is born with. The Manifestations of God are born with the knowledge of all created things.

lineage - Direct descent from an ancestor.

Manifestations of God – Prophets or Messengers from God. The word "manifest" means to become apparent, to show, or demonstrate. Therefore a Manifestation of God demonstrates God's attributes.

mosque - A Muslim place of worship.

Muslim - A follower of the Prophet Muhammad and His religion Islám.

Palestine - A territory in the Middle East, on the eastern coast of the Mediterranean Sea. Part of it is known today as Israel.

Persia - A former country of southwestern Asia, now called Iran. Its head of state was the s<u>h</u>áh.

pilgrimage - A journey - made by pilgrims - to a place of religious importance.

Prime Minister - The head of an elected government, the principal minister of a sovereign or state.

Proclamation - The public or official announcement of an important matter. Bahá'u'lláh's Proclamation refers to His announcement that He was a Manifestation of God.

Progressive Revelation of God – The word "progressive" means to happen or develop gradually or in stages. Therefore the phrase "Progressive Revelation of God" refers to how God reveals Himself to humanity from time to time.

Prophet - A person regarded as an inspired teacher or proclaimer of the will of God.

purity - Freedom from contamination.

Ottoman Empire - The Turkish Empire, established in northern Anatolia by Osman I at the end of the 13th century and expanded by his successors to include all of Asia Minor and much of southeastern Europe. It declined by the 19th century and collapsed after the First World War. Its head of state was the sulṭán.

retirement - To withdraw or seclude oneself.

revelation - Making something known through divine inspiration.

Sacred Writings - The word "sacred" means connected with God or dedicated to a religious purpose and so deserving veneration. Regarded with great respect and reverence by a particular religion, group, or individual. Therefore Sacred Writings or Sacred Teachings refers to writings or teachings that are revealed by God's Messengers.

stocks - An instrument of punishment consisting of an adjustable wooden structure with holes for securing a person's feet and hands, in which criminals were locked and exposed to public ridicule or assault.

tablet - A letter or epistle.

táj - A tall hat or tall conical cap.

The Universal House of Justice - The international governing council of the Bahá'í Faith. Its creation was ordained by Bahá'u'lláh.

veil - A piece of fine material worn by women to protect or conceal the face and/or hair as a sign of modesty.

victory - A moment of joy when the forces of evil have been defeated.

For further information about the Bahá'í Faith, please visit:

www.bahai.org

References:

`Abdu'l-Bahá, *Memorials of the Faithful*
Adib Taherzadeh, *The Revelation of Bahá'u'lláh*
Baharieh Rouhani Ma'ani, *Leaves of the Twin Divine Trees*
Bahá'í World Centre, *Visiting Bahá'í Holy Places*
Bahá'u'lláh, *Gleanings from the Writings of Bahá'u'lláh*
Bahá'u'lláh, *Tabernacle of Unity*
Bahá'u'lláh, *Bahá'í Prayers*
Bahá'u'lláh, *Epistle to the Son of the Wolf*
Bahá'u'lláh, *Tablets of Bahá'u'lláh*
Bahá'u'lláh, *Tablet of Carmel*
Bahá'u'lláh, *Kitáb-i-Aqdas*
Bahá'u'lláh, *Kitáb-i-Íqán*
Earl Redman, *'Abdu'l-Baha in Their Midst*
Helen Bassett Hornby, *Lights of Guidance*
H.M. Balyuzi, *Bahá'u'lláh: the King of Glory*
Janet A. Khan, *Prophet's Daughter*
J. E. Esslemont, *Bahá'u'lláh and the New Era*
Kaiser Barnes, *Stories of Bahá'u'lláh and Other Notable Believers*
Oxford Dictionary
Ruhi Institute, *Book 4: The Twin Manifestations*
Shoghi Effendi, *God Passes By*
Shoghi Effendi, *The Dawn-Breakers: Nabíl's Narrative of the Early Days of the Bahá'í Revelation*
Shoghi Effendi, *The World Order of Bahá'u'lláh*
Shoghi Effendi, *The Promised Day is Come*

Heartfelt thanks to:

My beloved husband Darioush Charepoo for all his support.
Leanna Guillén Mora for editing the book and helping with proofreading.
Sophia Wood, Alexandra Yazdani, and other contributors for helping with proofreading.

www.ingramcontent.com/pod-product-compliance
Lightning Source LLC
Chambersburg PA
CBHW041458120626
46547CB00003B/468